Waking Dream

July 1987

In my waking dream of you
    at the blonde slit of a burning dawn
Our hearts thud
    like apples falling in a darkened orchard
Our bodies stir
    like moist blossoms at first light
Pendulous with desire
    the quick wet musk of your
Mingles with
    the thick white gush of my forest rain

July 1987

A red moon splashes up
    over blackend boughs
Cicadas wail
Crushed violets feel cold
    under the paws of barking dogs.

I miss you incredibly.
I hold a sensual image of you in memory.
Can you hear me barking?

The Wedding Poem
3 July 1988

Only a moment ago
        my blue heart beat in an empty chest

Now crimson churning
        with violent jet

Deep as time my love for you

Hawaiian Honeymoon
5 July 1988

Until the clot of death
lies heavy on your hard lips

May my love
like a diamond
cut through your soul
and let the light shine out

July 1988

The cool breath of upland falls
   streams gaily from the lungs of the volcano
Falls like blood from a wound
   to the flash and swirl of waves

The lowing of island gods
   falls nakedly
   upon the bright caps of video haoles

The grunt of my soul
   as it clasps the inner thigh of yours
Falls perfectly through your
   deep-sea eyes
   to the foundations of paradise

July 1988

Thieves of love
racked on a bed of ecstasy
writhing in creamy slathering

Substantially
between the breath of eternity

Imprisoned in time
Paroled by the moon

Valentines Day 1989

Lithe as water.

Supple as earth.
Clear as the air.
Real as flame,

Our dream of love.

Valentine's Day 1990

No temporal flower
though it beauteous be,
Can match my
timeless love for Thee.

July 1990

Like two mooning clams are we
snug on the floor of a happy sea.
Shimmering, starlit sky above
below, bright hope, a sea of love.

Valentine's Day 1991

Hymn of Stone
Chant of Waves
A thousand Tongues
of a thousand Birds

All in your song.

Valentine's Day 1992

I see the years slip by,
like counting stones on the bottom of
a clear running stream,
their smoothness shimmering
in the light.

I hold you in my dreams,
tactile and surreal
and forever.

Remembering our Hawaiian
honeymoon on Valentine's Day 1993

Love of my life,
adorable wife,

Through the years ahead
we shall lightly tread
the sweet path of love

Never to part.

Valentine's Day 1994

As long as the trees
will hold their leafy burdens
aloft,

As long as the birds
will sing with unlikely chorus,
echoing down the
long paths of the trade winds,

As long as ice gnaws stone
in places we will never see,

So long as this
shall I love you.

Valentine's Day 1995

Under the tall wedding tree
hung with bright lights,
between the cicadas wail,
we sang our song of love.

Now, in the dying light
of a distant day;
with a young heart
and grateful soul

I sing that song again.

July 1998

Like-minded are we,
hearts
beating as one.

Forever we'll be
as diamonds,
never undone.

Valentine's Day 2001

The prairie winds blow
both ways

West at dawn to the
great blue rind of the ocean
stretched like a
rippled hide over
the huge fruit of the world

East at twilight
over the seeded mane of
the sighing plains

Until we come at last
to our one True Home

Valentine's Day 2002

Evensong spills briefly
from the tongues of
unseen birds.

Night air breathes heavily,
over darkened desert hills.

Echoes of our lovemaking
under the palms

Where I hold you
forever

Perfect and still.

July 2002

Full fourteen years have
swiftly flown,
Though gentle as a dove

Still Love's first kiss
seems but yesterday

And always will, my love.

July 2003

If I could choose again,
from all the paths as numerous
as summer leaves,
As unknown and fearful as
the midnight sun

Would I choose you, my love,
for my lifelong mate,
to be with me to watch the
sun slide down the long path of days,
Wallowing in its dusky redness?

To smile with me at a young boy's
morning stirrings and share his
young maturity?

As surely as the song of evening birds, and
the surge of tides, my love, and as truly.

July 2004

Upon the sea's broad
rippled breast

Our little bark

Tossed by the tides
of adversity

Becalmed by tedium

Yet still

Our floating paradise

Valentine's Day 2005

I tend the apple orchard,
as I always have.

With each practiced cut
another branch falls
to the mounting pile below.

In a winter's last barren stillness
the new iris thrust gently upwards.

The westering sun blinds me,

I call your name.

Valentine's Day 2006

A bell sounds in a high place
Its tone echoes in broad snowfields
illuminated by bright sunlight.

In the valley below
cherry blossoms fall and mingle,
one like another,
in muted darkling streams.

It takes practiced legs
and a strong back
to scale the mountain and visit
with its lofty muse
whose song, freely given,
lights all the world.

Valentine's Day 2007

A crane stands in a darkling stream,
still as memory.

Countless fingerlings rush past in
the cold water

Their clear flesh casting no shadow
on the speckled stones below.

At a soft cry overhead from
its mate
It springs silently aloft,
four wings, one heart.

Valentine's Day 2008

Whispers echo in a womb of countless nights,
promises and confession.
Your soft breath fuels my unsighted visions,
blind as air.

Births and deaths, unknowable joy
and black sorrow.
Our searching fingers till our constant garden,
real as earth.

Tears and rain, years of rapt baptisms.
Our bark surges ever towards the final shore,
sweet as water.

Bodies and minds, dancing like quasars.
Bound between void and infinite light,
Bright as enduring flame.

Valentine's Day 2009

Yesterday waits like
leaves in snow,
glimmering quietly.

Now, through sudden
immovable tears,
I see our perfect love,
as pebbles in clear
flowing water.

Valentine's Day 2010

A cold rain slides down
a changeling sky

Seven fledglings flock in
the plum tree outside my window

Their deep and stalwart black eyes
timeless and real

As our love

Valentine's Day 2011

In a calm twilight
under a waning moon
we have become like water
over smooth stones

two orphans in love

Valentine's Day 2012

A predawn breeze
flickers through
glowering leaves

Pale stars fade away
in the halflight
one by one

This day begins as
any other

But not quite

Our love blooms
like the rising sun

July 2012

When I touch your hand
    or stroke your hair

My heart jumps
    and births my devotion

Outside my window
    the sun blooms
    and the simple blades of grass
    twist and swirl in its radiance

And the secret and arcane truth
    that resides in the heart of all things

Suddenly becomes ordinary

Valentine's Day 2013

The evening breeze rises
in the East

Your smile shines upon me
in the curve at a new moon

A chorus of our love sounds
in the vesper prayers of
darkling birdsong

My embrace adores you
in a mantle of soft starlight

July 2013

Plum blossoms glow
in the sun

Our laughter
like the clatter of
old stones

www.ingramcontent.com/pod-product-compliance
Ingram Content Group UK Ltd.
Pitfield, Milton Keynes, MK11 3LW, UK
UKHW020227250726
13967UKWH00001B/226